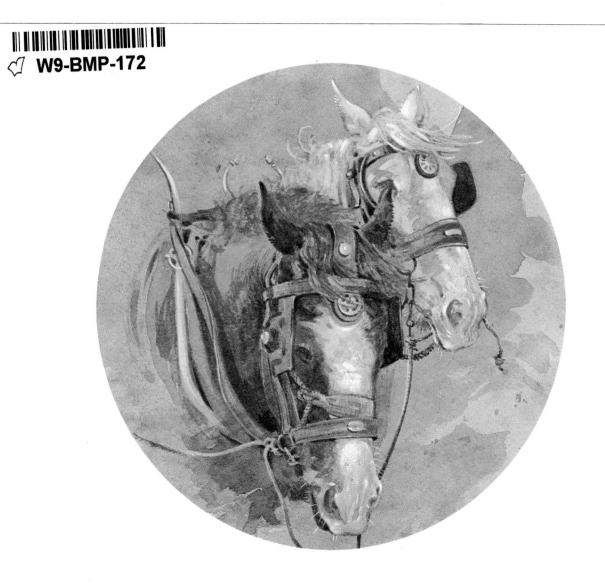

The Darkling Thrush

and other poems by
THOMAS HARDY

pictures by
GORDON BENINGFIELD

Viking

VIKING

Penguin Books Ltd,
Harmondsworth, Middlesex, England
Viking Penguin Inc.,
40 West 23rd Street, New York, New York 10010, U.S.A.
Penguin Books Australia Ltd,
Ringwood, Victoria, Australia
Penguin Books Canada Ltd,
2801 John Street, Markham, Ontario, Canada L3R 1B4
Penguin Books (N.Z.) Ltd,
182-190 Wairau Road, Auckland 10, New Zealand

First published 1985

Designed and selected by Ian Cameron and Jill Hollis
Produced by Cameron Books,
2a Roman Way, London N7 8XG

Filmset in Linotype Baskerville by Cameron Books
Printed in Holland by Royal Smeets Offset, Weert

British Library Cataloguing in Publication Data available

ISBN 0-670-80680-3

Poems

Pictures

Domicilium

It faces west, and round the back and sides
High beeches, bending, hang a veil of boughs,
And sweep against the roof. Wild honeysucks
Climb on the walls, and seem to sprout a wish
(If we may fancy wish of trees and plants)
To overtop the apple-trees hard by.

Red roses, lilacs, variegated box
Are there in plenty, and such hardy flowers
As flourish best untrained. Adjoining these
Are herbs and esculents; and farther still
A field; then cottages with trees, and last
The distant hills and sky.

Behind, the scene is wilder. Heath and furze
Are everything that seems to grow and thrive
Upon the uneven ground. A stunted thorn
Stands here and there, indeed; and from a pit
An oak uprises, springing from a seed
Dropped by some bird a hundred years ago.

                                    In days bygone –
Long gone – my father's mother, who is now
Blest with the blest, would take me out to walk.
At such a time I once inquired of her
How looked the spot when first she settled here.
The answer I remember. 'Fifty years
Have passed since then, my child, and change has marked
The face of all things. Yonder garden-plots
And orchards were uncultivated slopes
O'ergrown with bramble bushes, furze and thorn:
That road a narrow path shut in by ferns,
Which, almost trees, obscured the passer-by.

'Our house stood quite alone, and those tall firs
And beeches were not planted. Snakes and efts
Swarmed in the summer days, and nightly bats
Would fly about our bedrooms. Heathcroppers
Lived in the hills, and were our only friends;
So wild it was when first we settled here.'

Neutral Tones

We stood by a pond that winter day,
And the sun was white, as though chidden of God,
And a few leaves lay on the starving sod;
    – They had fallen from an ash, and were gray

Your eyes on me were as eyes that rove
Over tedious riddles of years ago;
And some words played between us to and fro
    On which lost the more by our love.

The smile on your mouth was the deadest thing
Alive enough to have strength to die;
And a grin of bitterness swept thereby
    Like an ominous bird a-wing . . .

Since then, keen lessons that love deceives,
And wrings with wrong, have shaped to me
Your face, and the God-curst sun, and a tree,
    And a pond edged with grayish leaves.

1867

Middle-Age Enthusiasms

To M.H.

We passed where flag and flower
Signalled a jocund throng;
We said: 'Go to, the hour
Is apt!' – and joined the song;
And, kindling, laughed at life and care,
Although we knew no laugh lay there.

We walked where shy birds stood
Watching us, wonder-dumb;
Their friendship met our mood;
We cried: 'We'll often come:
We'll come morn, noon, eve, everywhen!'
– We doubted we should come again.

We joyed to see strange sheens
Leap from quaint leaves in shade;
A secret light of greens
They'd for their pleasure made.
We said: 'We'll set such sorts as these!'
– We knew with night the wish would cease.

'So sweet the place,' we said,
'Its tacit tales so dear,
Our thoughts, when breath has sped,
Will meet and mingle here!' . . .
'Words!' mused we. 'Passed the mortal door,
Our thoughts will reach this nook no more.'

Nature's Questioning

When I look forth at dawning, pool,
    Field, flock, and lonely tree,
    All seem to gaze at me
Like chastened children sitting silent in a school;

Their faces dulled, constrained, and worn,
    As though the master's ways
    Through the long teaching days
Had cowed them till their early zest was overborne.

Upon them stirs in lippings mere
    (As if once clear in call,
    But now scarce breathed at all) –
'We wonder, ever wonder, why we find us here!

'Has some Vast Imbecility,
    Mighty to build and blend,
    But impotent to tend,
Framed us in jest, and left us now to hazardry?

'Or come we of an Automaton
    Unconscious of our pains? . . .
    Or are we live remains
Of Godhead dying downwards, brain and eye now gone?

'Or is it that some high Plan betides,
    As yet not understood,
    Of Evil stormed by Good,
We the Forlorn Hope over which Achievement strides?'

Thus things around. No answerer I . . .
    Meanwhile the winds, and rains,
    And Earth's old glooms and pains
Are still the same, and Life and Death are neighbours nigh.

A Commonplace Day

The day is turning ghost,
And scuttles from the kalendar in fits and furtively,
    To join the anonymous host
Of those that throng oblivion; ceding his place, maybe,
    To one of like degree.

    I part the fire-gnawed logs,
Rake forth the embers, spoil the busy flames, and lay the ends
    Upon the shining dogs;
Further and further from the nooks the twilight's stride extends,
    And beamless black impends.

    Nothing of tiniest worth
Have I wrought, pondered, planned; no one thing asking blame
    or praise,
    Since the pale corpse-like birth
Of this diurnal unit, bearing blanks in all its rays –
    Dullest of dull-hued Days!

    Wanly upon the panes
The rain slides, as have slid since morn my colourless thoughts;
    and yet
    Here, while Day's presence wanes,
And over him the sepulchre-lid is slowly lowered and set,
    He wakens my regret.

    Regret – though nothing dear
That I wot of, was toward in the wide world at his prime,
    Or bloomed elsewhere than here,
To die with his decease, and leave a memory sweet, sublime,
    Or mark him out in Time . . .

    – Yet, maybe, in some soul,
In some spot undiscerned on sea or land, some impulse rose,
    Or some intent upstole
Of that enkindling ardency from whose maturer glows
    The world's amendment flows;

    But which, benumbed at birth
By momentary chance or wile, has missed its hope to be
    Embodied on the earth;
And undervoicings of this loss to man's futurity
    May wake regret in me.

The Bullfinches

Brother Bulleys, let us sing
From the dawn till evening! –
For we know not that we go not
　　When to-day's pale pinions fold
　　Where they be that sang of old.

When I flew to Blackmoor Vale,
Whence the green-gowned faeries hail,
Roosting near them I could hear them
　　Speak of queenly Nature's ways,
　　Means, and moods, – well known to fays.

All we creatures, nigh and far
(Said they there), the Mother's are;
Yet she never shows endeavour
　　To protect from warrings wild
　　Bird or beast she calls her child.

Busy in her handsome house
Known as Space, she falls a-drowse;
Yet, in seeming, works on dreaming,
　　While beneath her groping hands
　　Fiends make havoc in her bands.

How her hussif'ry succeeds
She unknows or she unheeds,
All things making for Death's taking!
　　– So the green-gowned faeries say
　　Living over Blackmoor way.

Come then, brethren, let us sing,
From the dawn till evening! –
For we know not that we go not
　　When the day's pale pinions fold
　　Where those be that sang of old.

On a Fine Morning

I

Whence comes Solace? – Not from seeing
What is doing, suffering, being,
Not from noting Life's conditions,
Nor from heeding Time's monitions;
    But in cleaving to the Dream,
    And in gazing at the gleam
    Whereby gray things golden seem.

II

Thus do I this heyday, holding
Shadows but as lights unfolding,
As no specious show this moment
With its iris-hued embowment;
    But as nothing other than
    Part of a benignant plan;
    Proof that earth was made for man.   *February 1899*

22

Long Plighted

Is it worth while, dear, now,
To call for bells, and sally forth arrayed
For marriage-rites – discussed, descried, delayed
     So many years?

Is it worth while, dear, now,
To stir desire for old fond purposings,
By feints that Time still serves for dallyings,
     Though quittance nears?

Is it worth while, dear, when
The day being so far spent, so low the sun,
The undone thing will soon be as the done,
     And smiles as tears?

Is it worth while, dear, when
Our cheeks are worn, our early brown is gray;
When, meet or part we, none says yea or nay,
     Or heeds, or cares?

Is it worth while, dear, since
We still can climb old Yell'ham's wooded mounds
Together, as each season steals its rounds
     And disappears?

Is it worth while, dear, since
As mates in Mellstock churchyard we can lie,
Till the last crash of all things low and high
     Shall end the spheres?

An August Midnight

I

A shaded lamp and a waving blind,
And the beat of a clock from a distant floor:
On this scene enter – winged, horned, and spined –
A longlegs, a moth, and a dumbledore;
While 'mid my page there idly stands
A sleepy fly, that rubs its hands . . .

II

Thus meet we five, in this still place,
At this point of time, at this point in space.
– My guests besmear my new-penned line,
Or bang at the lamp and fall supine.
'God's humblest, they!' I muse. Yet why?
They know Earth-secrets that know not I.

Max Gate, 1899

Birds at Winter Nightfall

(Triolet)

Around the house the flakes fly faster,
And all the berries now are gone
From holly and cotonea-aster
Around the house. The flakes fly! – faster
Shutting indoors that crumb-outcaster
We used to see upon the lawn
Around the house. The flakes fly faster,
And all the berries now are gone!

Max Gate

The Puzzled Game-Birds

(Triolet)

They are not those who used to feed us
When we were young – they cannot be –
These shapes that now bereave and bleed us?
They are not those who used to feed us,
For did we then cry, they would heed us.
– If hearts can house such treachery
They are not those who used to feed us
When we were young – they cannot be!

24

The Caged Thrush Freed and Home Again

(Villanelle)

'Men know but little more than we,
Who count us least of things terrene,
How happy days are made to be!

'Of such strange tidings what think ye,
O birds in brown that peck and preen?
Men know but little more than we!

'When I was borne from yonder tree
In bonds to them, I hoped to glean
How happy days are made to be,

'And want and wailing turned to glee;
Alas, despite their mighty mien
Men know but little more than we!

'They cannot change the Frost's decree,
They cannot keep the skies serene;
How happy days are made to be

'Eludes great Man's sagacity
No less than ours, O tribes in treen!
Men know but little more than we
How happy days are made to be.'

The Last Chrysanthemum

Why should this flower delay so long
    To show its tremulous plumes?
Now is the time of plaintive robin-song,
    When flowers are in their tombs.

Through the slow summer, when the sun
    Called to each frond and whorl
That all he could for flowers was being done,
    Why did it not uncurl?

It must have felt that fervid call
    Although it took no heed,
Waking but now, when leaves like corpses fall,
    And saps all retrocede.

Too late its beauty, lonely thing,
    The season's shine is spent,
Nothing remains for it but shivering
    In tempests turbulent.

Had it a reason for delay,
    Dreaming in witlessness
That for a bloom so delicately gay
    Winter would stay its stress?

– I talk as if the thing were born
    With sense to work its mind;
Yet it is but one mask of many worn
    By the Great Face behind.

The Tenant-for-Life

The sun said, watching my watering-pot:
    'Some morn you'll pass away;
These flowers and plants I parch up hot –
    Who'll water them that day?

'Those banks and beds whose shape your eye
    Has planned in line so true,
New hands will change, unreasoning why
    Such shape seemed best to you.

'Within your house will strangers sit,
    And wonder how first it came;
They'll talk of their schemes for improving it,
    And will not mention your name.

'They'll care not how, or when, or at what
    You sighed, laughed, suffered here,
Though you feel more in an hour of the spot
    Than they will feel in a year.

'As I look on at you here, now,
    Shall I look on at these;
But as to our old times, avow
    No knowledge – hold my peace! . . .

'O friend, it matters not, I say;
    Bethink ye, I have shined
On nobler ones than you, and they
    Are dead men out of mind!'

The Darkling Thrush

I leant upon a coppice gate
    When Frost was spectre-gray,
And Winter's dregs made desolate
    The weakening eye of day.
The tangled bine-stems scored the sky
    Like strings of broken lyres,
And all mankind that haunted nigh
    Had sought their household fires.

The land's sharp features seemed to be
    The Century's corpse outleant,
His crypt the cloudy canopy,
    The wind his death-lament.
The ancient pulse of germ and birth
    Was shrunken hard and dry,
And every spirit upon earth
    Seemed fervourless as I.

At once a voice arose among
    The bleak twigs overhead
In a full-hearted evensong
    Of joy illimited;
An aged thrush, frail, gaunt, and small,
    In blast-beruffled plume,
Had chosen thus to fling his soul
    Upon the growing gloom.

So little cause for carolings
    Of such ecstatic sound
Was written on terrestrial things
    Afar or nigh around,
That I could think there trembled through
    His happy good-night air
Some blessed Hope, whereof he knew
    And I was unaware.

31 December 1900

The Milkmaid

Under a daisied bank
There stands a rich red ruminating cow,
And hard against her flank
A cotton-hooded milkmaid bends her brow.

The flowery river-ooze
Upheaves and falls; the milk purrs in the pail;
Few pilgrims but would choose
The peace of such a life in such a vale.

The maid breathes words – to vent,
It seems, her sense of Nature's scenery,
Of whose life, sentiment,
And essence, very part itself is she.

She bends a glance of pain,
And, at a moment, lets escape a tear;
Is it that passing train,
Whose alien whirr offends her country ear? –

Nay! Phyllis does not dwell
On visual and familiar things like these;
What moves her is the spell
Of inner themes and inner poetries:

Could but by Sunday morn
Her gay new gown come, meads might dry to dun,
Trains shriek till ears were torn,
If Fred would not prefer that Other One.

The Seasons of Her Year

I

Winter is white on turf and tree,
And birds are fled;
But summer songsters pipe to me,
And petals spread,
For what I dreamt of secretly
His lips have said!

II

O 'tis a fine May morn, they say,
And blooms have blown;
But wild and wintry is my day,
My song-birds moan;
For he who vowed leaves me to pay
Alone – alone!

In Tenebris I

'Percussus sum sicut fœnum, et aruit cor meum.' – Ps. CI

Wintertime nighs;
But my bereavement-pain
It cannot bring again:
    Twice no one dies.

Flower-petals flee;
But, since it once hath been,
No more that severing scene
    Can harrow me.

Birds faint in dread:
I shall not lose old strength
In the lone frost's black length:
    Strength long since fled!

Leaves freeze to dun;
But friends can not turn cold
This season as of old
    For him with none.

Tempests may scath;
But love can not make smart
Again this year his heart
    Who no heart hath.

Black is night's cope;
But death will not appal
One who, past doubtings all,
    Waits in unhope.

The Lost Pyx

A Medieval Legend

On a lonely table-land above the Vale of Blackmore, between High-Stoy and Bubb-Down hills, and commanding in clear weather views that extend from the English to the Bristol Channel, stands a pillar, apparently medieval, called Cross-and-Hand, or Christ-in-Hand. One tradition of its origin is mentioned in *Tess of the d'Urbervilles*; another, more detailed, preserves the story here given.

Some say the spot is banned: that the pillar Cross-and-Hand
    Attests to a deed of hell;
But of else than of bale is the mystic tale
    That ancient Vale-folk tell.

Ere Cernel's Abbey ceased hereabout there dwelt a priest,
    (In later life sub-prior
Of the brotherhood there, whose bones are now bare
    In the field that was Cernel choir).

One night in his cell at the foot of yon dell
    The priest heard a frequent cry:
'Go, father, in haste to the cot on the waste,
    And shrive a man waiting to die.'

Said the priest in a shout to the caller without,
    'The night howls, the tree-trunks bow;
One may barely by day track so rugged a way,
    And can I then do so now?'

No further word from the dark was heard,
    And the priest moved never a limb;
And he slept and dreamed; till a Visage seemed
    To frown from Heaven at him.

In a sweat he arose; and the storm shrieked shrill,
    And smote as in savage joy;
While High-Stoy trees twanged to Bubb-Down Hill,
    And Bubb-Down to High-Stoy.

There seemed not a holy thing in hail,
    Nor shape of light or love,
From the Abbey north of Blackmore Vale
    To the Abbey south thereof.

Yet he plodded thence through the dark immense,
    And with many a stumbling stride
Through copse and briar climbed nigh and nigher
    To the cot and the sick man's side.

When he would have unslung the Vessels uphung
    To his arm in the steep ascent,
He made loud moan: the Pyx was gone
    Of the Blessed Sacrament.

Then in dolorous dread he beat his head:
    'No earthly prize or pelf
Is the thing I've lost in tempest tossed,
    But the Body of Christ Himself!'

He thought of the Visage his dream revealed,
    And turned towards whence he came,
Hands groping the ground along foot-track and field,
    And head in a heat of shame.

Till here on the hill, betwixt vill and vill,
    He noted a clear straight ray
Stretching down from the sky to a spot hard by,
    Which shone with the light of day.

And gathered around the illumined ground
    Were common beasts and rare,
All kneeling at gaze, and in pause profound
    Attent on an object there.

'Twas the Pyx, unharmed 'mid the circling rows
    Of Blackmore's hairy throng,
Whereof were oxen, sheep, and does,
    And hares from the brakes among;

And badgers grey, and conies keen,
    And squirrels of the tree,
And many a member seldom seen
    Of Nature's family.

The ireful winds that scoured and swept
    Through coppice, clump, and dell,
Within that holy circle slept
    Calm as in hermit's cell.

Then the priest bent likewise to the sod
    And thanked the Lord of Love,
And Blessed Mary, Mother of God,
    And all the saints above.

And turning straight with his priceless freight,
    He reached the dying one,
Whose passing sprite had been stayed for the rite
    Without which bliss hath none.

And when by grace the priest won place,
    And served the Abbey well,
He reared this stone to mark where shone
    That midnight miracle.

Tess's Lament

I

I would that folk forgot me quite,
      Forgot me quite!
I would that I could shrink from sight,
      And no more see the sun.
Would it were time to say farewell,
To claim my nook, to need my knell,
Time for them all to stand and tell
      Of my day's work as done.

II

Ah! dairy where I lived so long,
      I lived so long;
Where I would rise up staunch and strong,
      And lie down hopefully.
'Twas there within the chimney-seat
He watched me to the clock's slow beat –
Loved me, and learnt to call me Sweet,
      And whispered words to me.

III

And now he's gone; and now he's gone; . . .
      And now he's gone!
The flowers we potted perhaps are thrown
      To rot upon the farm.
And where we had our supper-fire
May now grow nettle, dock, and briar,
And all the place be mould and mire
      So cozy once and warm.

IV

And it was I who did it all,
      Who did it all;
'Twas I who made the blow to fall
      On him who thought no guile,
Well, it is finished – past, and he
Has left me to my misery,
And I must take my Cross on me
      For wronging him awhile.

V

How gay we looked that day we wed,
      That day we wed!
'May joy be with ye!' they all said
      A-standing by the durn.
I wonder what they say o'us now,
And if they know my lot; and how
She feels who milks my favourite cow,
      And takes my place at churn!

VI

It wears me out to think of it,
      To think of it;
I cannot bear my fate as writ,
      I'd have my life unbe;
Would turn my memory to a blot,
Make every relic of me rot,
My doings be as they were not,
      And gone all trace of me!

The House of Hospitalities

Here we broached the Christmas barrel,
    Pushed up the charred log-ends;
Here we sang the Christmas carol,
      And called in friends.

Time has tired me since we met here
    When the folk now dead were young,
Since the viands were outset here
      And quaint songs sung.

And the worm has bored the viol
    That used to lead the tune,
Rust eaten out the dial
      That struck night's noon.

Now no Christmas brings in neighbours,
    And the New Year comes unlit;
Where we sang the mole now labours,
      And spiders knit.

Yet at midnight if here walking,
    When the moon sheets wall and tree,
I see forms of old time talking,
    Who smile on me.

The Farm-Woman's Winter

I

If seasons all were summers,
    And leaves would never fall,
And hopping casement-comers
    Were foodless not at all,
And fragile folk might be here
    That white winds bid depart;
Then one I used to see here
    Would warm my wasted heart!

II

One frail, who, bravely tilling
    Long hours in gripping gusts,
Was mastered by their chilling,
    And now his ploughshare rusts.
So savage winter catches
    The breath of limber things,
And what I love he snatches,
    And what I love not, brings.

From Her in the Country

I thought and thought of thy crass clanging town
To folly, till convinced such dreams were ill,
I held my heart in bond, and tethered down
Fancy to where I was, by force of will.

I said: How beautiful are these flowers, this wood,
One little bud is far more sweet to me
Than all man's urban shows; and then I stood
Urging new zest for bird, and bush, and tree;

And strove to feel my nature brought it forth
Of instinct, or no rural maid was I;
But it was vain; for I could not see worth
Enough around to charm a midge or fly,

And mused again on city din and sin,
Longing to madness I might move therein!

16 Westbourne Park Villas, 1866

A Church Romance

(Mellstock: circa 1835)

She turned in the high pew, until her sight
Swept the west gallery, and caught its row
Of music-men with viol, book, and bow
Against the sinking sad tower-window light.

She turned again; and in her pride's despite
One strenuous viol's inspirer seemed to throw
A message from his string to her below,
Which said: 'I claim thee as my own forthright!'

Thus their hearts' bond began, in due time signed.
And long years thence, when Age had scared Romance,
At some old attitude of his or glance
That gallery-scene would break upon her mind,
With him as minstrel, ardent, young, and trim,
Bowing 'New Sabbath' or 'Mount Ephraim'.

The Orphaned Old Maid

I wanted to marry, but father said, 'No –
'Tis weakness in women to give themselves so;
If you care for your freedom you'll listen to me,
Make a spouse in your pocket, and let the men be.'

I spake on't again and again: father cried,
'Why – if you go husbanding, where shall I bide?
For never a home's for me elsewhere than here!'
And I yielded; for father had ever been dear.

But now father's gone, and I feel growing old,
And I'm lonely and poor in this house on the wold,
And my sweetheart that was found a partner elsewhere,
And nobody flings me a thought or a care.

By the Barrows

Not far from Mellstock – so tradition saith –
Where barrows, bulging as they bosoms were
Of Multimammia stretched supinely there,
Catch night and noon the tempest's wanton breath,

A battle, desperate doubtless unto death,
Was one time fought. The outlook, lone and bare,
The towering hawk and passing raven share,
And all the upland round is called 'The He'th'.

Here once a woman, in our modern age,
Fought singlehandedly to shield a child –
One not her own – from a man's senseless rage.
And to my mind no patriots' bones there piled
So consecrate the silence as her deed
Of stoic and devoted self-unheed.

47

The Roman Road

The Roman Road runs straight and bare
As the pale parting-line in hair
Across the heath. And thoughtful men
Contrast its days of Now and Then,
And delve, and measure, and compare;

Visioning on the vacant air
Helmed legionaries, who proudly rear
The Eagle, as they pace again
       The Roman Road.

But no tall brass-helmed legionnaire
Haunts it for me. Uprises there
A mother's form upon my ken,
Guiding my infant steps, as when
We walked that ancient thoroughfare,
       The Roman Road.

To Sincerity

O sweet sincerity! –
Where modern methods be
What scope for thine and thee?

Life may be sad past saying,
Its greens for ever graying,
Its faiths to dust decaying;

And youth may have foreknown it,
And riper seasons shown it,
But custom cries: 'Disown it:

'Say ye rejoice, though grieving,
Believe, while unbelieving,
Behold, without perceiving!'

– Yet, would men look at true things
And unilluded view things,
And count to bear undue things,

The real might mend the seeming,
Facts better their foredeeming,
And Life its disesteeming.

February 1899

Channel Firing

That night your great guns, unawares,
Shook all our coffins as we lay,
And broke the chancel window-squares,
We thought it was the Judgment-day

And sat upright. While drearisome
Arose the howl of wakened hounds:
The mouse let fall the altar-crumb,
The worms drew back into the mounds,

The glebe cow drooled. Till God called, 'No;
It's gunnery practice out at sea
Just as before you went below;
The world is as it used to be:

'All nations striving strong to make
Red war yet redder. Mad as hatters
They do no more for Christés sake
Than you who are helpless in such matters.

'That this is not the judgment-hour
For some of them's a blessed thing,
For if it were they'd have to scour
Hell's floor for so much threatening . . .

'Ha, ha. It will be warmer when
I blow the trumpet (if indeed
I ever do; for you are men,
And rest eternal sorely need).'

So down we lay again, 'I wonder,
Will the world ever saner be,'
Said one, 'than when He sent us under
In our indifferent century!'

And many a skeleton shook his head.
'Instead of preaching forty year,'
My neighbour Parson Thirdly said,
'I wish I had stuck to pipes and beer.'

Again the guns disturbed the hour,
Roaring their readiness to avenge,
As far inland as Stourton Tower,
And Camelot, and starlit Stonehenge.

April 1914

51

A Thunderstorm in Town

(A Reminiscence: 1893)

She wore a new 'terra-cotta' dress,
And we stayed, because of the pelting storm,
Within the hansom's dry recess,
Though the horse had stopped; yea, motionless
    We sat on, snug and warm.

Then the downpour ceased, to my sharp sad pain,
And the glass that had screened our forms before
Flew up, and out she sprang to her door:
I should have kissed her if the rain
    Had lasted a minute more.

When I Set Out for Lyonnesse

(1870)

When I set out for Lyonnesse,
    A hundred miles away,
    The rime was on the spray,
And starlight lit my lonesomeness
When I set out for Lyonnesse
    A hundred miles away.

What would bechance at Lyonnesse
    While I should sojourn there
    No prophet durst declare,
Nor did the wisest wizard guess
What would bechance at Lyonnesse
    While I should sojourn there.

When I came back from Lyonnesse
    With magic in my eyes,
    All marked with mute surmise
My radiance rare and fathomless,
When I came back from Lyonnesse
    With magic in my eyes!

Wessex Heights

(1896)

There are some heights in Wessex, shaped as if by a kindly hand
For thinking, dreaming, dying on, and at crises when I stand,
Say, on Ingpen Beacon eastward, or on Wylls-Neck westwardly,
I seem where I was before my birth, and after death may be.

In the lowlands I have no comrade, not even the lone man's friend –
Her who suffereth long and is kind; accepts what he is too weak
    to mend:
Down there they are dubious and askance; there nobody thinks as I,
But mind-chains do not clank where one's next neighbour is the sky.

In the towns I am tracked by phantoms having weird detective ways –
Shadows of beings who fellowed with myself of earlier days:
They hang about at places, and they say harsh heavy things –
Men with a wintry sneer, and women with tart disparagings.

Down there I seem to be false to myself, my simple self that was,
And is not now, and I see him watching, wondering what crass cause
Can have merged him into such a strange continuator as this,
Who yet has something in common with himself, my chrysalis.

I cannot go to the great grey Plain; there's a figure against the moon,
Nobody sees it but I, and it makes my breast beat out of tune;
I cannot go to the tall-spired town, being barred by the forms
    now passed
For everybody but me, in whose long vision they stand there fast.

There's a ghost at Yell'ham Bottom chiding loud at the fall of
    the night,
There's a ghost in Froom-side Vale, thin-lipped and vague, in a
    shroud of white,
There is one in the railway train whenever I do not want it near,
I see its profile against the pane, saying what I would not hear.

As for one rare fair woman, I am now but a thought of hers,
I enter her mind and another thought succeeds me that she prefers;
Yet my love for her in its fulness she herself even did not know;
Well, time cures hearts of tenderness, and now I can let her go.

So I am found on Ingpen Beacon, or on Wylls-Neck to the west,
Or else on homely Bulbarrow, or little Pilsdon Crest,
Where men have never cared to haunt, nor women have walked
    with me,
And ghosts then keep their distance; and I know some liberty.

Before and after Summer

I

Looking forward to the spring
One puts up with anything.
On this February day
Though the winds leap down the street
Wintry scourgings seem but play,
And these later shafts of sleet
– Sharper pointed than the first –
And these later snows – the worst –
Are as a half-transparent blind
Riddled by rays from sun behind.

II

Shadows of the October pine
Reach into this room of mine:
On the pine there swings a bird;
He is shadowed with the tree.
Mutely perched he bills no word;
Blank as I am even is he.
For those happy suns are past,
Fore-discerned in winter last.
When went by their pleasure, then?
I, alas, perceived not when.

At Day-Close in November

The ten hours' light is abating,
    And a late bird wings across,
Where the pines, like waltzers waiting,
    Give their black heads a toss.

Beech leaves, that yellow the noon-time,
    Float past like specks in the eye;
I set every tree in my June time,
    And now they obscure the sky.

And the children who ramble through here
    Conceive that there never has been
A time when no tall trees grew here,
    That none will in time be seen.

The Walk

You did not walk with me
Of late to the hill-top tree
    By the gated ways,
    As in earlier days;
    You were weak and lame,
    So you never came,
And I went alone, and I did not mind,
Not thinking of you as left behind.

I walked up there to-day
Just in the former way;
    Surveyed around
    The familiar ground
    By myself again:
    What difference, then?
Only that underlying sense
Of the look of a room on returning thence.

Without Ceremony

It was your way, my dear,
To vanish without a word
When callers, friends, or kin
Had left, and I hastened in
To rejoin you, as I inferred.

And when you'd a mind to career
Off anywhere – say to town –
You were all on a sudden gone
Before I had thought thereon,
Or noticed your trunks were down.

So, now that you disappear
For ever in that swift style,
Your meaning seems to me
Just as it used to be:
'Good-bye is not worth while!'

After a Journey

Hereto I come to view a voiceless ghost;
    Whither, O whither will its whim now draw me?
Up the cliff, down, till I'm lonely, lost,
    And the unseen waters' ejaculations awe me.
Where you will next be there's no knowing,
    Facing round about me everywhere,
        With your nut-coloured hair,
And gray eyes, and rose-flush coming and going.

Yes: I have re-entered your olden haunts at last;
    Through the years, through the dead scenes I have tracked you;
What have you now found to say of our past –
    Scanned across the dark space wherein I have lacked you?
Summer gave us sweets, but autumn wrought division?
    Things were not lastly as firstly well
        With us twain, you tell?
But all's closed now, despite Time's derision.

I see what you are doing: you are leading me on
    To the spots we knew when we haunted here together,
The waterfall, above which the mist-bow shone
    At the then fair hour in the then fair weather,
And the cave just under, with a voice still so hollow
    That it seems to call out to me from forty years ago,
        When you were all aglow,
And not the thin ghost that I now fraily follow!

Ignorant of what there is flitting here to see,
    The waked birds preen and the seals flop lazily;
Soon you will have, Dear, to vanish from me,
    For the stars close their shutters and the dawn whitens hazily.

Trust me, I mind not, though Life lours,
    The bringing me here; nay, bring me here again!
    I am just the same as when
Our days were a joy, and our paths through flowers.

The Voice ·

Woman much missed, how you call to me, call to me,
Saying that now you are not as you were
When you had changed from the one who was all to me,
But as at first, when our day was fair.

Can it be you that I hear? Let me view you, then,
Standing as when I drew near to the town
Where you would wait for me: yes, as I knew you then,
Even to the original air-blue gown!

Or is it only the breeze, in its listlessness
Travelling across the wet mead to me here,
Yŏu being ever dissolved to wan wistlessness,
Heard no more again far or near?

    Thus I; faltering forward,
    Leaves around me falling,
Wind oozing thin through the thorn from norward,
    And the woman calling.

December 1912

Afternoon Service at Mellstock

(Circa 1850)

On afternoons of drowsy calm
    We stood in the panelled pew,
Singing one-voiced a Tate-and-Brady psalm
    To the tune of 'Cambridge New'.

We watched the elms, we watched the rooks,
    The clouds upon the breeze,
Between the whiles of glancing at our books,
    And swaying like the trees.

So mindless were those outpourings! –
    Though I am not aware
That I have gained by subtle thought on things
    Since we stood psalming there.

Great Things

Sweet cyder is a great thing,
  A great thing to me,
Spinning down to Weymouth town
  By Ridgway thirstily,
And maid and mistress summoning
  Who tend the hostelry:
O cyder is a great thing,
  A great thing to me!

The dance it is a great thing,
  A great thing to me,
With candles lit and partners fit
  For night-long revelry;
And going home when day-dawning
  Peeps pale upon the lea:
O dancing is a great thing,
  A great thing to me!

Love is, yea, a great thing,
  A great thing to me,
When, having drawn across the lawn
  In darkness silently,
A figure flits like one a-wing
  Out from the nearest tree:
O love is, yes, a great thing,
  A great thing to me!

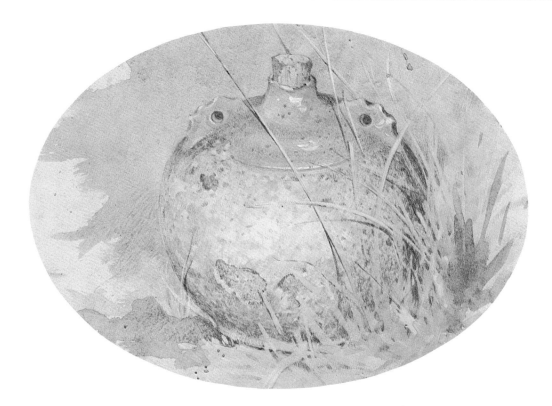

Will these be always great things,
  Great things to me? . . .
Let it befall that One will call,
  'Soul, I have need of thee:'
What then? Joy-jaunts, impassioned flings,
  Love, and its ecstasy,
Will always have been great things,
  Great things to me!

At Tea

The kettle descants in a cosy drone,
And the young wife looks in her husband's face,
And then at her guest's, and shows in her own
Her sense that she fills an envied place;
And the visiting lady is all abloom,
And says there was never so sweet a room.

And the happy young housewife does not know
That the woman beside her was first his choice,
Till the fates ordained it could not be so . . .
Betraying nothing in look or voice
The guest sits smiling and sips her tea,
And he throws her a stray glance yearningly.

On a Heath

I could hear a gown-skirt rustling
    Before I could see her shape,
Rustling through the heather
    That wove the common's drape,
On that evening of dark weather
    When I hearkened, lips agape.

And the town-shine in the distance
    Did but baffle here the sight,
And then a voice flew forward:
    'Dear, is't you? I fear the night!'
And the herons flapped to norward
    In the firs upon my right.

There was another looming
    Whose life we did not see;
There was one stilly blooming
    Full nigh to where walked we;
There was a shade entombing
    All that was bright of me.

The House of Silence

'That is a quiet place –
That house in the trees with the shady lawn.'
' – If, child, you knew what there goes on
You would not call it a quiet place.
Why, a phantom abides there, the last of its race,
    And a brain spins there till dawn.'

'But I see nobody there, –
Nobody moves about the green,
Or wanders the heavy trees between.'
' – Ah, that's because you do not bear
The visioning powers of souls who dare
    To pierce the material screen.

'Morning, noon, and night,
Mid those funereal shades that seem
The uncanny scenery of a dream,
Figures dance to a mind with sight,
And music and laughter like floods of light
    Make all the precincts gleam.

'It is a poet's bower,
Through which there pass, in fleet arrays,
Long teams of all the years and days,
Of joys and sorrows, of earth and heaven,
That meet mankind in its ages seven,
    An aion in an hour.'

Why Did I Sketch?

Why did I sketch an upland green,
    And put the figure in
    Of one on the spot with me? –
For now that one has ceased to be seen
    The picture waxes akin
    To a wordless irony.

If you go drawing on down or cliff
    Let no soft curves intrude
    Of a woman's silhouette,
But show the escarpments stark and stiff
    As in utter solitude;
    So shall you half forget.

Let me sooner pass from sight of the sky
    Than again on a thoughtless day
    Limn, laugh, and sing, and rhyme
With a woman sitting near, whom I
    Paint in for love, and who may
    Be called hence in my time!

From an old note

At Middle-Field Gate in February

The bars are thick with drops that show
    As they gather themselves from the fog
Like silver buttons ranged in a row,
And as evenly spaced as if measured, although
    They fall at the feeblest jog.

They load the leafless hedge hard by,
    And the blades of last year's grass,
While the fallow ploughland turned up nigh
In raw rolls, clammy and clogging lie –
    Too clogging for feet to pass.

How dry it was on a far-back day
    When straws hung the hedge and around,
When amid the sheaves in amorous play
In curtained bonnets and light array
    Bloomed a bevy now underground!

Bockhampton Lane

Logs on the Hearth

A Memory of a Sister

The fire advances along the log
    Of the tree we felled,
Which bloomed and bore striped apples by the peck
    Till its last hour of bearing knelled.

The fork that first my hand would reach
    And then my foot
In climbings upward inch by inch, lies now
    Sawn, sapless, darkening with soot.

Where the bark chars is where, one year,
    It was pruned, and bled –
Then overgrew the wound. But now, at last,
    Its growings all have stagnated.

My fellow-climber rises dim
    From her chilly grave –
Just as she was, her foot near mine on the bending limb,
    Laughing, her young brown hand awave.

December 1915

A Backward Spring

The trees are afraid to put forth buds,
And there is timidity in the grass;
The plots lie gray where gouged by spuds,
    And whether next week will pass
Free of sly sour winds is the fret of each bush
    Of barberry waiting to bloom.

Yet the snowdrop's face betrays no gloom,
And the primrose pants in its heedless push,
Though the myrtle asks if it's worth the fight
    This year with frost and rime
    To venture one more time
On delicate leaves and buttons of white
From the selfsame bough as at last year's prime,
And never to ruminate on or remember
What happened to it in mid-December.

April 1917

79

Paths of Former Time

No; no;
It must not be so:
They are the ways we do not go.

Still chew
The kine, and moo
In the meadows we used to wander through;

Still purl
The rivulets and curl
Towards the weirs with a musical swirl;

Haymakers
As in former years
Rake rolls into heaps that the pitchfork rears;

Wheels crack
On the turfy track
The waggon pursues with its toppling pack.

'Why then shun –
Since summer's not done –
All this because of the lack of one?'

Had you been
Sharer of that scene
You would not ask while it bites in keen

Why it is so
We can no more go
By the summer paths we used to know!

1913

While Drawing in a Churchyard

'It is sad that so many of worth,
  Still in the flesh,' soughed the yew,
'Misjudge their lot whom kindly earth
  Secludes from view.

'They ride their diurnal round
  Each day-span's sum of hours
In peerless ease, without jolt or bound
  Or ache like ours.

'If the living could but hear
  What is heard by my roots as they creep
Round the restful flock, and the things said there,
  No one would weep.'

' "Now set among the wise,"
  They say: "Enlarged in scope,
That no God trumpet us to rise
  We truly hope." '

I listened to his strange tale
  In the mood that stillness brings,
And I grew to accept as the day wore pale
  That show of things.

The Pity of It

I walked in loamy Wessex lanes, afar
From rail-track and from highway, and I heard
In field and farmstead many an ancient word
Of local lineage like 'Thu bist', 'Er war',

'Ich woll', 'Er sholl', and by-talk similar,
Nigh as they speak who in this month's moon gird
At England's very loins, thereunto spurred
By gangs whose glory threats and slaughters are.

Then seemed a Heart crying: 'Whosoever they be
At root and bottom of this, who flung this flame
Between kin folk kin tongued even as are we,

'Sinister, ugly, lurid, be their fame;
May their familiars grow to shun their name,
And their brood perish everlastingly.'

April 1915

In Time of 'The Breaking of Nations'

I

Only a man harrowing clods
   In a slow silent walk
With an old horse that stumbles and nods
   Half asleep as they stalk.

II

Only thin smoke without flame
   From the heaps of couch-grass;
Yet this will go onward the same
   Though Dynasties pass.

III

Yonder a maid and her wight
   Come whispering by:
War's annals will cloud into night
   Ere their story die.

1915

Afterwards

When the Present has latched its postern behind my tremulous stay,
   And the May month flaps its glad green leaves like wings,
Delicate-filmed as new-spun silk, will the neighbours say,
   'He was a man who used to notice such things'?

If it be in the dusk when, like an eyelid's soundless blink,
   The dewfall-hawk comes crossing the shades to alight
Upon the wind-warped upland thorn, a gazer may think,
   'To him this must have been a familiar sight.'

If I pass during some nocturnal blackness, mothy and warm,
   When the hedgehog travels furtively over the lawn,
One may say, 'He strove that such innocent creatures should come to no harm,
   But he could do little for them; and now he is gone.'

If, when hearing that I have been stilled at last, they stand at the door,
   Watching the full-starred heavens that winter sees,
Will this thought rise on those who will meet my face no more,
   'He was one who had an eye for such mysteries'?

And will any say when my bell of quittance is heard in the gloom,
   And a crossing breeze cuts a pause in its outrollings,
Till they rise again, as they were a new bell's boom,
   'He hears it not now, but used to notice such things'?

Weathers

I

This is the weather the cuckoo likes,
    And so do I;
When showers betumble the chestnut spikes,
    And nestlings fly:
And the little brown nightingale bills his best,
And they sit outside at 'The Travellers' Rest',
And maids come forth sprig-muslin drest,
And citizens dream of the south and west,
    And so do I.

II

This is the weather the shepherd shuns,
    And so do I;
When beeches drip in browns and duns,
    And thresh, and ply;
And hill-hid tides throb, throe on throe,
And meadow rivulets overflow,
And drops on gate-bars hang in a row,
And rooks in families homeward go,
    And so do I.

The West-of-Wessex Girl

A very West-of-Wessex girl,
   As blithe as blithe could be,
   Was once well-known to me,
And she would laud her native town,
   And hope and hope that we
Might sometime study up and down
   Its charms in company.

But never I squired my Wessex girl
   In jaunts to Hoe or street
   When hearts were high in beat,
Nor saw her in the marbled ways
   Where market-people meet
That in her bounding early days
   Were friendly with her feet.

Yet now my West-of-Wessex girl,
   When midnight hammers slow
   From Andrew's, blow by blow,
As phantom draws me by the hand
   To the place – Plymouth Hoe –
Where side by side in life, as planned,
   We never were to go!

Begun in Plymouth, March 1913

Epeisodia

I

Past the hills that peep
Where the leaze is smiling,
On and on beguiling
Crisply-cropping sheep;
Under boughs of brushwood
Linking tree and tree
In a shade of lushwood,
    There caressed we!

II

Hemmed by city walls
That outshut the sunlight,
In a foggy dun light,
Where the footstep falls
With a pit-pat wearisome
In its cadency
On the flagstones drearisome
    There pressed we!

III

Where in wild-winged crowds
Blown birds show their whiteness
Up against the lightness
Of the clammy clouds;
By the random river
Pushing to the sea,
Under bents that quiver
    There shall rest we.

If It's Ever Spring Again

(Song)

If it's ever spring again,
    Spring again,
I shall go where went I when
Down the moor-cock splashed, and hen,
Seeing me not, amid their flounder,
Standing with my arm around her;
If it's ever spring again,
    Spring again,
I shall go where went I then.

If it's ever summer-time,
    Summer-time,
With the hay crop at the prime,
And the cuckoos – two – in rhyme,
As they used to be, or seemed to,
We shall do as long we've dreamed to,
If it's ever summer-time,
    Summer-time,
With the hay, and bees achime.

Saying Good-bye

(Song)

We are always saying
   'Good-bye, good-bye!'
In work, in playing,
In gloom, in gaying:
   At many a stage
   Of pilgrimage
   From youth to age
   We say, 'Good-bye,
    Good-bye!'

We are undiscerning
   Which go to sigh,
Which will be yearning
For soon returning;
   And which no more
   Will dark our door,
   Or tread our shore,
   But go to die,
    To die.

Some come from roaming
   With joy again;
Some, who come homing
By stealth at gloaming,
   Had better have stopped
   Till death, and dropped
   By strange hands propped,
   Than come so fain,
    So fain.

So, with this saying,
   'Good-bye, good-bye,'
We speed their waying
Without betraying
   Our grief, our fear
   No more to hear
   From them, close, clear,
   Again: 'Good-bye,
    Good-bye!'

The Selfsame Song

A bird sings the selfsame song,
With never a fault in its flow,
That we listened to here those long
    Long years ago.

A pleasing marvel is how
A strain of such rapturous rote
Should have gone on thus till now
    Unchanged in a note!

– But it's not the selfsame bird. –
No: perished to dust is he . . .
As also are those who heard
    That song with me.

Growth in May

I enter a daisy-and-buttercup land,
    And thence thread a jungle of grass:
Hurdles and stiles scarce visible stand
    Above the lush stems as I pass.

Hedges peer over, and try to be seen,
    And seem to reveal a dim sense
That amid such ambitious and elbow-high green
    They make a mean show as a fence.

Elsewhere the mead is possessed of the neats,
    That range not greatly above
The rich rank thicket which brushes their teats,
    And *her* gown, as she waits for her Love.

Near Chard

A House with a History

There is a house in a city street
  Some past ones made their own;
Its floors were criss-crossed by their feet,
    And their babblings beat
  From ceiling to white hearth-stone.

And who are peopling its parlours now?
  Who talk across its floor?
Mere freshlings are they, blank of brow,
    Who read not how
  Its prime had passed before.

Their raw equipments, scenes, and says
  Afflicted its memoried face,
That had seen every larger phase
    Of human ways
  Before these filled the place.

To them that house's tale is theirs,
  No former voices call
Aloud therein. Its aspect bears
    Their joys and cares
  Alone, from wall to wall.

Best Times

We went a day's excursion to the stream,
Basked by the bank, and bent to the ripple-gleam,
    And I did not know
    That life would show,
However it might flower, no finer glow.

I walked in the Sunday sunshine by the road
That wound towards the wicket of your abode,
    And I did not think
    That life would shrink
To nothing ere it shed a rosier pink.

Unlooked for I arrived on a rainy night,
And you hailed me at the door by the swaying light,
    And I full forgot
    That life might not
Again be touching that ecstatic height.

And that calm eve when you walked up the stair,
After a gaiety prolonged and rare,
    No thought soever
    That you might never
Walk down again, struck me as I stood there.

Rewritten from an old draft

Last Week in October

The trees are undressing, and fling in many places –
On the gray road, the roof, the window-sill –
Their radiant robes and ribbons and yellow laces;
A leaf each second so is flung at will,
Here, there, another and another, still and still.

A spider's web has caught one while downcoming,
That stays there dangling when the rest pass on;
Like a suspended criminal hangs he, mumming
In golden garb, while one yet green, high yon,
Trembles, as fearing such a fate for himself anon.

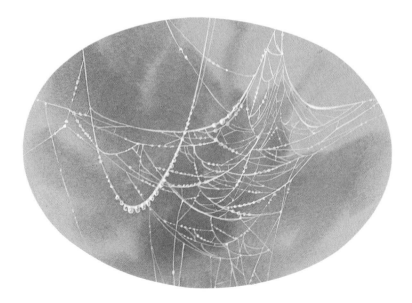

The Later Autumn

Gone are the lovers, under the bush
    Stretched at their ease;
    Gone the bees,
Tangling themselves in your hair as they rush
    On the line of your track,
    Leg-laden, back
    With a dip to their hive
    In a prepossessed dive.

Toadsmeat is mangy, frosted, and sere;
    Apples in grass
    Crunch as we pass,
And rot ere the men who make cyder appear.
    Couch-fires abound
    On fallows around,
    And shades far extend
    Like lives soon to end.

Spinning leaves join the remains shrunk and brown
    Of last year's display
    That lie wasting away,
On whose corpses they earlier as scorners gazed down
    From their aery green height:
    Now in the same plight
    They huddle; while yon
    A robin looks on.

A Sheep Fair

The day arrives of the autumn fair,
    And torrents fall,
Though sheep in throngs are gathered there,
    Ten thousand all,
Sodden, with hurdles round them reared:
And, lot by lot, the pens are cleared,
And the auctioneer wrings out his beard,
And wipes his book, bedrenched and smeared,
And rakes the rain from his face with the edge of his hand,
    As torrents fall.

The wool of the ewes is like a sponge
    With the daylong rain:
Jammed tight, to turn, or lie, or lunge,
    They strive in vain.
Their horns are soft as finger-nails,
Their shepherds reek against the rails,
The tied dogs soak with tucked-in tails,
The buyers' hat-brims fill like pails,
Which spill small cascades when they shift their stand
    In the daylong rain.

POSTSCRIPT

Time has trailed lengthily since met
    At Pummery Fair
Those panting thousands in their wet
    And woolly wear:
And every flock long since has bled,
And all the dripping buyers have sped,
And the hoarse auctioneer is dead,
Who 'Going – going!' so often said,
As he consigned to doom each meek, mewed band
    At Pummery Fair.

The Weary Walker

A plain in front of me,
   And there's the road
Upon it. Wide country,
   And, too, the road!

Past the first ridge another,
   And still the road
Creeps on. Perhaps no other
   Ridge for the road?

Ah! Past that ridge a third,
   Which still the road
Has to climb furtherward –
   The thin white road!

Sky seems to end its track;
   But no. The road
Trails down the hill at the back.
   Ever the road!

When Oats Were Reaped

That day when oats were reaped, and wheat was ripe, and barley
      ripening,
  The road-dust hot, and the bleaching grasses dry,
    I walked along and said,
While looking just ahead to where some silent people lie:

'I wounded one who's there, and now know well I wounded her;
  But, ah, she does not know that she wounded me!'
    And not an air stirred,
Nor a bill of any bird; and no response accorded she.

August 1913

The Harvest-Supper

(Circa 1850)

Nell and the other maids danced their best
  With the Scotch-Greys in the barn;
These had been asked to the harvest-feast;
  Red shapes amid the corn.

Nell and the other maids sat in a row
  Within the benched barn-nook;
Nell led the songs of long ago
  She'd learnt from never a book.

She sang of the false Sir John of old,
  The lover who witched to win,
And the parrot, and cage of glittering gold;
  And the other maids joined in.

Then whispered to her a gallant Grey,
  'Dear, sing that ballet again!
For a bonnier mouth in a bonnier way
  Has sung not anywhen!'

As she loosed her lips anew there sighed
  To Nell through the dark barn-door
The voice of her Love from the night outside,
  Who was buried the month before:

'O Nell, can you sing ballets there,
  And I out here in the clay,
Of lovers false of yore, nor care
  What you vowed to me one day!

'O can you dance with soldiers bold,
  Who kiss when dancing's done,
Your little waist within their hold,
  As ancient troth were none!'

She cried: 'My heart is pierced with a wound!
  There's something outside the wall
That calls me forth to a greening mound:
  I can sing no more at all!

'My old Love rises from the worms,
  Just as he used to be,
And I must let gay gallants' arms
  No more encircle me!'

They bore her home from the merry-making;
  Bad dreams disturbed her bed:
'Nevermore will I dance and sing,'
  Mourned Nell; 'and never wed!'

I Watched a Blackbird

I watched a blackbird on a budding sycamore
One Easter Day, when sap was stirring twigs to the core;
   I saw his tongue, and crocus-coloured bill
   Parting and closing as he turned his trill;
   Then he flew down, seized on a stem of hay,
And upped to where his building scheme was under way,
As if so sure a nest were never shaped on spray.

Days to Recollect

Do you recall
　　That day in Fall
When we walked towards Saint Alban's Head,
On thistledown that summer had shed,
　　Or must I remind you?
Winged thistle-seeds which hitherto
Had lain as none were there, or few,
But rose at the brush of your petticoat-seam
(As ghosts might rise of the recent dead),
And sailed on the breeze in a nebulous stream
　　Like a comet's tail behind you:
　　You don't recall
　　That day in Fall?

　　Then do you remember
　　That sad November
When you left me never to see me more,
And looked quite other than theretofore,
　　As if it could not *be* you?
And lay by the window whence you had gazed
So many times when blamed or praised,
Morning or noon, through years and years,
Accepting the gifts that Fortune bore,
Sharing, enduring, joys, hopes, fears!
　　Well: I never more did see you. –
　　Say you remember
　　That sad November!

An Unkindly May

A shepherd stands by a gate in a white smock-frock:
He holds the gate ajar, intently counting his flock.

The sour spring wind is blurting boisterous-wise,
And bears on it dirty clouds across the skies;
Plantation timbers creak like rusty cranes,
And pigeons and rooks, dishevelled by late rains,
Are like gaunt vultures, sodden and unkempt,
And song-birds do not end what they attempt:
The buds have tried to open, but quite failing
Have pinched themselves together in their quailing.

The sun frowns whitely in eye-trying flaps
Through passing cloud-holes, mimicking audible taps.
'Nature, you're not commendable to-day!'
I think. 'Better to-morrow!' she seems to say.

That shepherd still stands in that white smock-frock,
Unnoting all things save the counting his flock.

Expectation and Experience

'I had a holiday once,' said the woman –
  Her name I did not know –
'And I thought that where I'd like to go,
Of all the places for being jolly,
And getting rid of melancholy,
  Would be to a good big fair:
And I went. And it rained in torrents, drenching
Every horse, and sheep, and yeoman,
  And my shoulders, face and hair;
And I found that I was the single woman
  In the field – and looked quite odd there!
Everything was spirit-quenching:
I crept and stood in the lew of a wall
To think, and could not tell at all
  What on earth made me plod there!'

We Field-Women

How it rained
When we worked at Flintcomb-Ash,
And could not stand upon the hill
Trimming swedes for the slicing-mill.
The wet washed through us – plash, plash, plash:
How it rained!

How it snowed
When we crossed from Flintcomb-Ash
To the Great Barn for drawing reed,
Since we could nowise chop a swede. –
Flakes in each doorway and casement-sash:
How it snowed!

How it shone
When we went from Flintcomb-Ash
To start at dairywork once more
In the laughing meads, with cows three-score,
And pails, and songs, and love – too rash:
How it shone!

Seeing the Moon Rise

We used to go to Froom-hill Barrow
     To see the round moon rise
     Into the heath-rimmed skies,
Trudging thither by plough and harrow
Up the pathway, steep and narrow,
     Singing a song.
Now we do not go there. Why?
     Zest burns not so high!

Latterly we've only conned her
     With a passing glance
     From window or door by chance,
Hoping to go again, high yonder,
As we used, and gaze, and ponder,
     Singing a song.
Thitherward we do not go:
     Feet once quick are slow!

August 1927

He Never Expected Much

[or]

A Consideration

[A reflection] on My Eighty-Sixth Birthday

Well, World, you have kept faith with me,
  Kept faith with me;
Upon the whole you have proved to be
  Much as you said you were.
Since as a child I used to lie
Upon the leaze and watch the sky,
Never, I own, expected I
  That life would all be fair.

'Twas then you said, and since have said,
  Times since have said,
In that mysterious voice you shed
  From clouds and hills around:
'Many have loved me desperately,
Many with smooth serenity,
While some have shown contempt of me
  Till they dropped underground.

'I do not promise overmuch,
  Child; overmuch;
Just neutral-tinted haps and such,'
  You said to minds like mine.
Wise warning for your credit's sake!
Which I for one failed not to take,
And hence could stem such strain and ache
  As each year might assign.

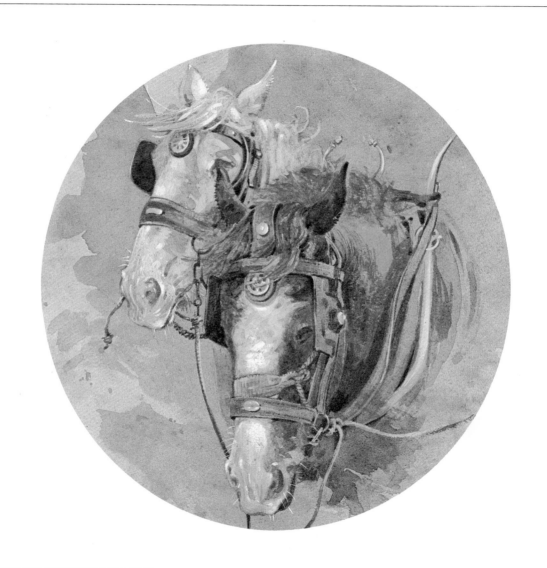